Incredible Amphibians

John Townsend

www.raintreepublishers.co.uk
Visit our website to find out more information about **Raintree** books.

To order:
☎ Phone 44 (0) 1865 888113
🖹 Send a fax to 44 (0) 1865 314091
🖥 Visit the Raintree Bookshop at **www.raintreepublishers.co.uk** to browse our catalogue and order online.

First published in Great Britain by Raintree Publishers,
Halley Court, Jordan Hill, Oxford, OX2 8EJ,
part of Harcourt Education Ltd.
Raintree is a registered trademark of Harcourt
Education Ltd.

Produced for Raintree Publishers by Discovery Books Ltd
Editorial: Louise Galpine, Sarah Jameson,
Charlotte Guillain, and Diyan Leake
Expert Reader: Jill Bailey
Design: Victoria Bevan, Keith Williams (sprout.uk.com
Limited), and Michelle Lisseter
Picture Research: Maria Joannou
Production: Duncan Gilbert and Jonathan Smith
Printed and bound in China by South China
Printing Company
Originated by Repro Multi Warna

ISBN 1 844 43453 2 (hardback)
09 08 07 06 05
10 9 8 7 6 5 4 3 2 1

ISBN 1 844 43473 7 (paperback)
09 08 07 06 05
10 9 8 7 6 5 4 3 2 1

British Library Cataloguing in Publication Data
Townsend, John
Incredible Amphibians. – (Incredible Creatures)
597.8
A full catalogue record for this book is available from the
British Library.

This levelled text is a version of Freestyle:
Incredible creatures: Incredible amphibians.

Photo acknowledgements
Bryan & Cherry Alexander p. **40** left; Corbis pp. **20** (Lynda
Richardson), **24** right (David A. Northcott), **42–3** (Phil
Schermeister), **48** bottom (Martin B. Withers/Frank Lane
Picture Agency), **51** (Fadek Timothy); Digital Vision pp. **5**
bottom, **32**; FLPA pp. **6** right (John Tinning), **7** (Michael
Clark), **8** right (Yossi Eshbol), **12** right (Albert Visage), **12**
left (Roger Wilmshurst), **13** (Minden Pictures), **16** (Alwyn
J. Roberts), **16–17** (Michael Clark), **18** bottom (Tony
Hamblin), **22** right (David Hosking), **24** left (Richard
Brooks), **26** right (Silvestris), **27** (G. Marcoaldi/Panda
Photos), **28** (Alwyn J. Roberts), **28–9** (Martin B. Withers),
30 left (B. Borrell), **31**, **33** (Minden Pictures), **40** right
(Chris Mattison), **47** (B. S. Turner); Getty Images p. **10**
right; Naturepl pp. **14** (Morley Read), **39** (Jose B. Ruiz), **46**
(Dietmar Nill); NHPA pp. **4**, **4–5** (Stephen Dalton), **5** top
(Stephen Dalton), **5** middle (Stephen Dalton), **6** left
(Stephen Dalton), **8** left (Rod Planck), **9** (National
Geographic), **10** left (Stephen Dalton), **11** (John Shaw),
14–15 (Daniel Heuclin), **15** (Jany Sauvanet), **18** top
(Stephen Dalton), **19** (G. I. Bernard), **20–1** (Stephen
Dalton), **21** (Stephen Dalton), **22** left (Daniel Heuclin), **26**
left (Daniel Heuclin), **29** (Stephen Dalton), **30** right (Ant
Photo Library), **34–5** (Robert Erwin), **36** (Ant Photo
Library), **36–7** (Daniel Heuclin), **37** (Ant Photo Library),
38 bottom (Stephen Dalton), **38** top (Ant Photo Library),
41 (Karl Switak), **43** (Stephen Dalton), **44** (Ralph &
Daphne Keller), **44–5** (Stephen Dalton), **48** top (Bill
Coster), **49** (Ant Photo Library), **50** (Stephen Dalton);
Oxford Scientific Films pp. **17** (David M. Dennis), **23** (Dess
& Jen Bartlett/FAL), **32–3** (Nick Gordon), **34** (Alan &
Sandy Carey), **42**; Photodisc p. **25**; Photofusion pp. **50–1**
(David Preston); Science Photo Library **45** (Dr Morley Read)
Cover photograph of a green frog reproduced with
permission of Science Photo Library (David N. Davis)

The Publishers would like to thank Jon Pearce for his
assistance in the preparation of this book. Every effort has
been made to contact copyright holders of any material
reproduced in this book. Any omissions will be rectified in
subsequent printings if notice is given to the Publishers.

Disclaimer
All the Internet addresses (URLs) given in this book were
valid at the time of going to press. However, due to the
dynamic nature of the Internet, some addresses may have
changed, or sites may have changed or ceased to exist since
publication. While the author and Publishers regret any
inconvenience this may cause readers, no responsibility for
any such changes can be accepted by either the author or
the Publishers.

Contents

Any words appearing in the text in bold, **like this**, are explained in the Glossary. You can also look out for some of them in the 'Wild words' bank at the bottom of each page.

The world of amphibians

Would you believe it?

Amphibians are some of the oldest animals on Earth. Scientists think they have been around for as long as 360 million years.

Did you know that amphibians live two lives? Most start their lives in water, as eggs. They hatch into wriggly **larvae** and swim around. Instead of lungs, they breathe through special flaps of skin called **gills**.

Growing legs

Then something amazing happens to young amphibians. They start to develop lungs, grow legs, and lose their wiggly tails! They climb out of the water and begin a new life on dry land.

▲ This amphibian has a long, thin body. It is a giant salamander.

larva (more than one are called larvae) young form of an
animal that is very different from the adult

Three groups

There are three main groups of amphibians:

- Frogs and toads belong to the largest group. There are over 3500 **species**.

- Newts and salamanders have long, thin bodies with tails. There are around 360 different species.

- **Caecilians** are strange amphibians. They have no legs and look like worms. Most live underground.

Find out later...

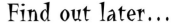

... what an axolotl is.

... how toads can live inside solid rock.

... how this frog can kill you.

▲ This common frog has strong back legs to help it jump.

species type of living animal or plant

Meet the family

Tiny tadpoles

A single frog can lay as many as 30,000 eggs at a time. You can see the eggs below are growing into tiny **larvae**. Frog and toad larvae are called **tadpoles**.

There are more than 4000 **species** of amphibian on Earth. In this chapter we will find out more about the three different groups of amphibian.

Frogs and toads

Frogs live all over the world except some deserts and islands. You have probably seen them in your garden or nearby pond.

▼ This common frog is swimming under water.

tadpole young stage, or larva, of a frog, toad, newt, or salamander

Frog or toad?

Frogs and toads are really the same animal, but if you look closely you will see some differences.

Frogs have smooth, wet skin. They have long back legs and are good at hopping.

Toads usually have drier, bumpier skin. They have short legs, which means they walk rather than hop.

Raining frogs?

Sometimes very strong **whirlwinds** can scoop up water from lakes. Tadpoles and frogs get sucked up too. Later it can actually rain tadpoles and frogs!

▼ An army of common frogs is on the march. They are hopping over the grass.

whirlwind column of air whirling round and round very fast

Great variety

Frogs and toads come in lots of different shapes, sizes, and colours.

Some live in holes they dig under the soil. Others live high in the tops of trees and can **glide** through the air. Most frogs and toads like to live on land close to water and some spend their whole lives in the water.

When is a toad not a toad?

When it is a lizard! The horned toad that you can see below is not a toad at all. It is a kind of lizard.

▼

▶ This is a green toad. Can you see its lumpy, bumpy skin?

glide float through the air

Poisonous!

Many frogs and toads have poisons in their skins.

Toads have special **glands** behind their eyes. If they are attacked, poison oozes out from these glands.

If a cat or a dog catches a toad, the poison can make it foam at the mouth. Some frogs and toads make poison strong enough to harm humans.

◀ Can you spot the frog among this group of toads?

gland part of the body that produces chemicals such as poisons or digestive juices

Big babies!

The axolotl (say 'acks-o-lot-ol') is a very strange salamander from Mexico.

Some axolotls grow into adults and live on land. Others never grow up and stay in the water.

Salamanders

Many salamanders look like lizards with smooth skins. They have lots of different shapes and sizes. Some salamanders are called newts.

Hellbenders

The strangely-named hellbender is a giant salamander. It has a large, heavy body and a short tail. Slimy and difficult to hold, it can grow longer than your arm. Hellbenders have many teeth, but they do not often try to bite humans.

▲ Hellbenders might look scary, but in fact they are harmless.

In or out of the water?

Some salamanders live on dry land and others spend their lives in the water.

Lungless salamanders live in damp places on land. They have no lungs and breathe through their skin.

Sirens are salamanders that live their whole life under water. They look like eels. Instead of lungs, they use **gills** for breathing.

Old salamanders

When kept in zoos or as pets, salamanders can live for up to 25 years. A few have lived for more than 50 years!

▼ Unlike frogs, salamanders keep their tail when they grow up. This is a long-tailed forest salamander from North America.

gills delicate, feathery structures that allow some animals to breathe under water

11

Newts

Newts are small salamanders (usually less than the width of this single page in size). They live mostly in water in the northern half of the world.

Like many salamanders, newts have four short legs and a long, strong tail. Newts hide in cool, damp places. They come out at night to feed on snails and insects. That is why we do not see them very often.

Warts and all

The great crested newt (shown below) is also called the warty newt. Males sometimes have a frill of skin along their back, called a crest.

▶ These brightly-coloured marbled newts live in parts of Europe.

Legs and tails

Like some lizards, newts can **shed**, or drop, their tails if something grabs them. This can help them to escape. After a while the newt just grows a new tail!

If a newt loses a leg, it can grow a new one in a few months. Scientists do not yet know how this happens, but it is very useful for the newt.

All change

When it is young, the eastern newt, shown below, is red in colour. It lives on land close to water. After two to three years, it returns to water and becomes a beautiful yellow and green adult.

shed get rid of, or lose

Long and short

There are around 160 different **species** of caecilian. The largest of them is around 1.5 metres (5 feet) long. That's about the length of a garden rake.

Caecilians

Unlike salamanders, frogs, and toads, **caecilians** have no legs. They have long, thin bodies and look like worms.

Caecilians live in warm parts of the world, such as the **tropical** forests of South America and Africa. They live out of sight, burrowing in the soil and mud, or swimming under water.

▼ A caecilian's skin has lots of folds. It can bend its body in any direction.

species type of living animal or plant

Slippery customers

Another name for caecilians is rubber eels. If you hold one, it feels like a smooth, rubbery tube. It often tries to tie itself into knots!

Tiny eyes

Although they have tiny eyes, many caecilians are blind. Two small **feelers** on their head help them to find insects and worms to eat.

Skin colours

Caecilians come in different colours. Some are blackish blue, some are pink, and others are orange. Some caecilians have spots or stripes.

◄ In its dark, muddy world, a caecilian does not need its eyes.

feeler little fleshy flap of skin used to smell, taste, or touch

Amazing bodies

Amphibians' bodies are amazing because they change completely as they grow.

Air and water

All animals need **oxygen** to live. They get this from the air or from water. Animals that live in water breathe with **gills**, like fish. Animals that live on land have lungs, like we do.

Gills and lungs

But how do amphibians cope if they live in water and on the land? Simple. They have both gills and lungs ... sometimes!

Growing up

Frogs have gills only when they are **tadpoles**. Look at the tadpoles below. Can you see the feathery gills on the side of their head?

Wild words   oxygen one of the gases in air and water that all living things need

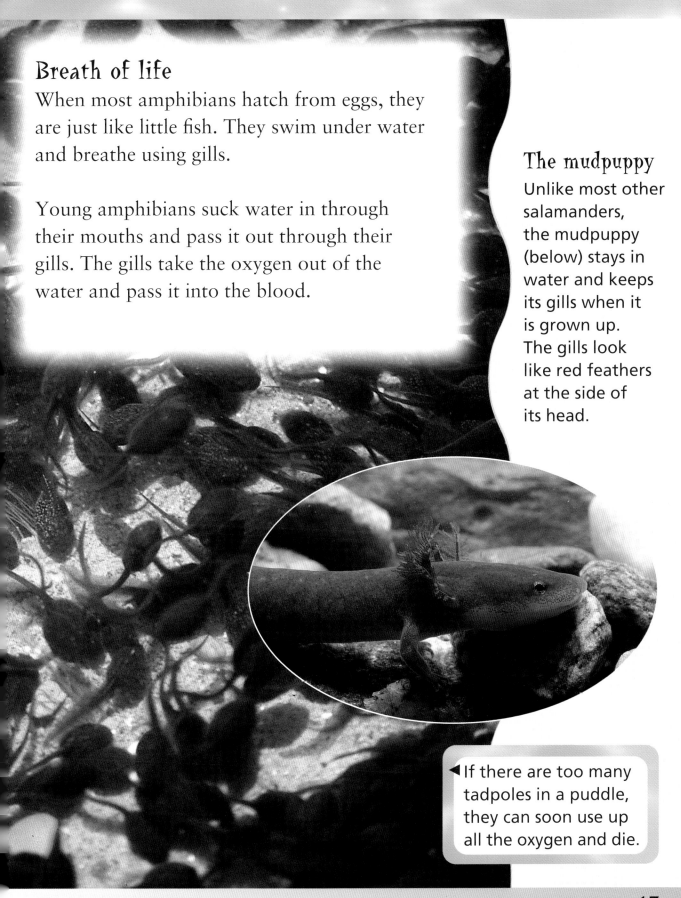

Breath of life

When most amphibians hatch from eggs, they are just like little fish. They swim under water and breathe using gills.

Young amphibians suck water in through their mouths and pass it out through their gills. The gills take the oxygen out of the water and pass it into the blood.

The mudpuppy

Unlike most other salamanders, the mudpuppy (below) stays in water and keeps its gills when it is grown up. The gills look like red feathers at the side of its head.

◄ If there are too many tadpoles in a puddle, they can soon use up all the oxygen and die.

Tadpole gills

Newly-hatched tadpoles have gills on the outside of their bodies. A cover of skin soon grows over the gills to protect them.

Living on land

As most amphibians grow into adults, their **gills** start to disappear. They grow lungs instead. This means they can breathe out of water.

Adult amphibians have another way of getting **oxygen** into their bodies. They can actually breathe through their skin. Amphibian skin is not **waterproof** like ours. It lets in water and oxygen.

▼ Common frogs do not need to drink. They can take in water through their skin.

gland part of the body that produces chemicals such as poisons or digestive juices

Amazing skin

Amphibians have **glands** in their skin that make slime. A coating of slime helps the skin to stay wet. It also helps the animal to breathe.

Keeping wet

It is very important for frogs that they do not dry out. Their skin lets water out as well as in. Frogs can easily lose too much water and die. This is why they usually live close to water.

Old skin

Frogs **shed** their skin regularly to keep it healthy. The frog wriggles out of the old skin, which comes off like a slimy vest. Then guess what? The frog eats it!

▼ This frog is swallowing its old skin. The skin contains **nutrients** that are good for it to eat.

nutrient substance found in food that is needed by the body to grow strong and healthy

Feeding

Salamander food

Salamanders living in water suck their prey into their mouths. On land, some salamanders feed like frogs. They flick out their sticky tongues to catch insects.

Most adult amphibians are **carnivores**. This means they hunt and eat other animals, called **prey**. They eat mostly insects, spiders, worms, and smaller amphibians.

Different amphibians have different ways of finding their food. **Caecilians** cannot see well. They sit and wait for a juicy worm to wriggle close by. Then they grab it with their sharp teeth.

◄ This red spotted newt is munching on a worm.

prey animal that is killed and eaten by other animals

Fast food

Unlike caecilians, frogs can leap for their food with long, strong legs.

Frogs can also see and hear well. They have long, sticky tongues. When they see an insect they want to eat, they can flick out their tongue in a flash. The tongue sticks to the insect and snaps back into the frog's mouth, fast.

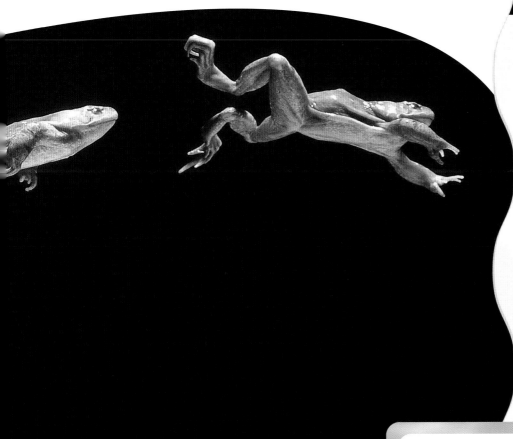

Sticky frog

The red-eyed tree frog (shown above) lives in **tropical** forests. With sticky pads on its toes it can grip on to leaves and branches.

◄ With one quick leap, a frog can catch insects to eat in mid-air.

Big appetites

Many toads have no teeth at all. They use their front feet to push food down into their throat. A single toad may eat 10,000 insects in one summer. That takes a lot of swallowing!

How frogs eat

Frogs have small teeth but they cannot chew their food like we can.

When a frog or toad swallows food it does something very strange. It closes its eyes and squeezes its eyeballs down into its head. This helps to push the food down its throat. Imagine having to do that to eat your dinner!

▼ An African bullfrog will eat just about anything it can get into its mouth.

Mouths on legs

Horned frogs are large and very colourful. They live in South America. They like to eat large insects, lizards, mice, and other frogs.

Horned frogs sit and wait for food to come near them before they attack. They have huge mouths that seem to take up the whole of their head.

Bad taste

Some frogs do not have to worry about what they eat. If it tastes bad or is poisonous, they can turn their stomach inside out through their mouth and wipe it clean!

▼ This horned frog is swallowing a mouse whole. What a mouthful!

Breeding

Newts on the move

In Washington State, USA, scientists did an experiment. They took lots of newts more than 1.5 kilometres (nearly 1 mile) away from their breeding pond. Guess what? Each newt found its way back to the pond.

Amphibians live alone for most of the year. To **breed** they must first get together.

Meeting up

When it is time to breed, amphibians have to find a partner. Frogs, toads, and salamanders use all sorts of tricks to attract each other. We do not know much about how **caecilians** meet.

▼ Newts return to the same pond to breed each year. These are red-spotted newts.

breed produce young

Looking for a mate

In the springtime, amphibians go out and look for a pond where they can **mate**. This is often the pond they were born in.

They sometimes travel to the breeding pond in large groups. This is a dangerous time for them because they have to cross roads and railway lines. They are often squashed by traffic. Sometimes they are killed by **predators**.

Huge numbers of amphibians gather at the pond ready to breed.

"I'm here!"

Male frogs and toads 'talk', or croak, to females by making a noise in their throat.

The common frogs below have gathered in a pool to breed. It is going to get very noisy!

◀ This male toad is not blowing bubble gum. He is croaking.

mate when a male and female animal come together to produce young

Mating

Many female amphibians lay hundreds of eggs at a time in water.

The male frog clings to the female's back as she lays her eggs. Frogs' eggs are called **frogspawn**. You may have seen frogspawn in your local pond in springtime. It looks like jelly.

Mating can last minutes or several days, depending on the type of frog.

Water dance

Newts and salamanders do not have voices like frogs and toads. Instead the male attracts the female by doing a dance for her in the water.

▼ Can you see all the eggs the frog has laid?

▲ The male Californian newt rubs his chin on the back of the female's head.

Eggs in jelly

Amphibian eggs do not have a shell to protect them like birds' eggs. Instead they are surrounded by clear jelly. It is very important that the eggs do not dry out. If they do, the tiny amphibians inside will die.

Amphibians will often lay many eggs because most of them will not **survive**. Eggs are a tasty meal for other animals, so many of them get eaten before they even have a chance to hatch.

Laying eggs

Many amphibians lay their eggs in water. Some lay their eggs in damp places on land. **Caecilians** lay eggs under leaves or rocks, or in cracks in the ground.

▼ These are salamander eggs. Look at the tiny, white **larvae** growing inside the jelly.

survive stay alive despite danger and difficulties

A big change

Amphibian young are amazing because they are completely different from their parents. They go through a huge change to become adults. This change is called **metamorphosis**.

From tadpole to frog

After a few days, frogs' eggs hatch into wriggly **larvae** called **tadpoles**.

A new tadpole has a mouth, tail, and feathery **gills** for breathing. But it does not stay like this for very long. Its body begins to make an amazing change from tadpole to adult frog.

▼ This is a common frog tadpole. It does not look much like a frog yet.

► Frogs have been busy laying eggs. Look at all this **frogspawn** in the water.

larva (more than one are called larvae) young form of an
animal that is very different from the adult

Growing fast

Before long, skin grows over the tadpole's gills.
Later, the back legs start to grow. Next come the
front legs. Then, the tail starts to shrink fast.
By now, the tadpole has lungs to gulp air and it
needs to come to the surface of the water to breathe.

Finally, the new frog is ready to leave the water
and begin a new life on land.

No hurry

Some frogs
live high up in
mountains or
in cold places.
Here, they may
spend the whole
winter as tadpoles.
The cold slows
everything down.

◄ This little frog has
nearly lost its tadpole
shape, but it still has
a stumpy tail.

frogspawn jelly-like mass of frogs' eggs

Caring for their young

Amphibian parents usually leave their young to look after themselves. But some frogs are more caring.

Mother care

The gastric-brooding frog lived in Australia until the early 1980s. The mother frog did an unusual thing. She swallowed her eggs and kept them in her stomach. There the eggs could grow up out of danger.

Egg carrier

The male **midwife** toad (shown below) has a clever way of looking after his young. He carries the eggs around on his back legs until they hatch and swim off.

▲ This is a gastric-brooding frog with one of her young, ready to hop out. Sadly these frogs are now **extinct**.

midwife nurse who helps babies to be born

Special care

Strawberry poison arrow frogs do not lay eggs in water, but on land. When the new **tadpoles** hatch, the mother carries them on her back to a tree. She finds small leaves filled with water for the tadpoles. They grow up in these tiny pools and the mother feeds them with spare eggs.

Foster parents?

Recently, scientists have found tadpoles in ants' nests, like the one below, in South America. The ants fed the tadpoles in watery pools under the nest. Maybe they were baby-sitting? No one knows for sure.

Father frogs

The Darwin's frog lives in South American streams. The male frog guards the eggs for two weeks. Then he swallows them. They grow in the baggy skin under his chin. When they are ready, they hop out.

extinct died out, never to return

Defence

Lots of animals like to eat amphibians. However, amphibians have many ways of protecting themselves against these **predators**.

Poisonous frogs

The tiny poison-arrow frogs of South America make a deadly poison. Small amounts of it can kill a human. The Amazon Indians have found a good use for this poison. They put it on the tips of their arrows for hunting animals. When they shoot a poisoned arrow into an animal, it dies very quickly.

Keep away!
The poison-arrow frog (below), has bright colours to warn off attackers. The colours say "keep away! I'm poisonous."

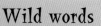

Useful poisons

The poison made by the golden poison-arrow frog (below) may one day be useful in medicine. Tiny amounts of this poison may help people who have heart problems.

Frog dangers

Poison-arrow frogs have many beautiful, bright colours. People take them from the wild and sell them as colourful pets. But beware! Anyone who touches these frogs could be in danger. If the poison gets into a cut you can die from an instant heart attack.

Poisonous newts

One way to stop something from eating you is to kill it first!

Handle with care

In 1979 a man from Oregon, USA, made a bet that he could safely eat a poisonous rough-skinned newt (shown below). He did not win the bet. He died soon after swallowing the newt.

Rough-skinned newts

Some newts have very poisonous skins. The rough-skinned newt lives in North America. It is one of the most poisonous salamanders of all. A single newt has enough poison in its body to kill 1500 mice. A tiny amount can even kill a human. There is no known **antidote** for this poison.

antidote medicine given to make a poison safe

Copying colours

The Californian newt from the USA is bright red and orange. These colours warn birds and snakes not to eat the newt.

The red salamander has bright colours too, but it is not poisonous at all. It **mimics**, or copies, the colours of the poisonous salamander. Although the red salamander is harmless, its colours send a warning message to **predators** to stay away. How sneaky is that?

Rock and roll

The Mount Lyell salamander lives under rocks in the mountains of California. It has an unusual way of protecting itself. If it is frightened, it curls into a ball and rolls away down the hillside!

◄ This red salamander is a bright colour, but it is not poisonous.

The deadly toad

The cane toad is the world's largest toad. It comes from South America.

In the 1930s, cane toads were brought to Australia, the Caribbean, and the USA to eat insects that were harming **sugar cane** plants. The cane toads did a good job. But then they began to take over. They ate almost anything.

Beware!

A big cane toad can squirt a jet of poison up to 30 centimetres (12 inches). The milky, foamy poison comes from behind the cane toad's head (see below).

► This cane toad is munching on a small snake.

sugar cane grassy plant that sugar comes from

Giant appetites

Cane toads have very big appetites. They gulp down insects such as beetles, crickets, and ants. They eat snails as well as other frogs and toads. They even eat honeybees! They eat pet food and household scraps if they are left outside.

With all this food, no wonder some cane toads grow nearly as big as your dinner plate!

Pet dangers

The skin of the cane toad has a deadly poison. It burns the lips of dogs or cats that pick the toad up in their mouth. They usually drop the toad right away. Just as well, because eating a cane toad would be a deadly mistake.

▲ This crowd of cane toads has gathered to catch insects that fly around street lamps at night.

Colour and camouflage

Looks are important if you are an amphibian. They can be a matter of life and death.

Some amphibians can change colour. One type of frog can live in the desert because of its colour. It changes from brown to white in bright sunlight. The white colour reflects the sun and stops the frog from getting sunburn.

Hiding with colour

Many amphibians have colours and patterns that blend in well with their surroundings. This sort of colouring is called **camouflage**. The burrowing frog (above) lives in the woodlands of Australia. Its greeny-brown colours make it difficult to see.

camouflage colours and patterns that match the background

Warning messages

Fire-bellied toads are green and black on their backs. They also have bright red-orange bellies, which warn **predators** that they are poisonous.

If frightened, the toad lifts its head and legs to flash these bold colours. This can scare a predator for a few moments. The toad then has a few seconds to make its escape.

Wriggling tails

Salamanders (see below) wave their tails around to confuse predators. They can also lose their tail altogether! The tail wriggles on the ground while the salamander runs away to grow a new one.

◄This fire-bellied toad has bright colours to scare any attackers.

Weird and wonderful

Although most amphibians need to live in wet places, some can **survive** hot deserts or icy places.

Frozen alive!

The North American wood frog survives extremely cold winters. Ice forms around its body. Its heart stops beating and its lungs stop working. But it does not die. The frog produces a kind of **anti-freeze** that keeps it alive. When the spring comes, the frog **thaws** out again.

Icy salamander

In snowy mountains like the ones below, the temperature can get as low as -50 °C (-58 °F). Amazingly, an amphibian called the Siberian salamander can live in this icy place.

anti-freeze liquid that does not freeze at temperatures below 0 °C (32 °F)

The long wait

Australian desert frogs have a hard time. It is very hot and very dry in the desert. It may not rain for 10 years. So how does the frog survive?

The frog burrows underground and waits. It lives on water it has stored in its body. When the rain finally comes it is time to wake up again.

Fit and healthy

The African clawed toad (shown below) lives in warm, still water full of **viruses**. The toad's skin makes a special substance that fights the viruses, so the toad stays fit and healthy.

▼ The Australian desert frog is sometimes called the water-holding frog.

virus very tiny creature that causes some diseases

Toad in the hole

In 1835 a man called John Bruton saw a big piece of rock fall off a wagon. It cracked open. Much to his surprise, out of the hole crawled a live toad!

Unsolved mystery

Some amphibians seem to be able to **survive** inside solid rock. Sometimes builders knock down old walls and find a toad sealed up inside.

In 1995 a schoolboy from Wales picked up a drink can. Inside was a frog, but mysteriously it was too big to get out.

So, how did these frogs and toads get there?

▲ Cane toads, like this one, turn up in all sorts of places.

Prisoner!

Drink cans and cracks in rocks are cool, damp places. Tiny, young frogs can wriggle into them. Insects also shelter in these places, so the frog can eat – and grow! As it grows, it gets trapped inside.

With water and a supply of food, a frog could live for years as a prisoner like this.

▼ In the past, frogs and toads have been seen as mysterious. They have been linked to magic and witches for hundreds of years.

◄ Cracks in rocks are good hiding places for amphibians.

Life in the trees

Some amphibians spend their lives in the tops of trees.

Many tree frogs never come down from the trees. They **mate** and lay their eggs high in the branches. When the **tadpoles** hatch they drop into the puddles below. But they climb back up again once they become adult frogs.

Tree frogs

There are around 800 **species** of tree frog (see below) that we know about. There may be many more tree frogs in the **rainforests** that we have not yet discovered.

► This Wallace's tree frog is 'flying' through the air. It is a very good way of escaping danger.

rainforest forest that grows in warm parts of the world where there is a lot of rainfall

Flying frogs

Some frogs can fly! Actually they **glide** rather than fly. Their four big feet have flaps of skin between the toes. The frogs spread their toes out like little **parachutes** as they jump from tree to tree.

Wallace's tree frog can glide up to 15 metres (nearly 50 feet) through the air. That is about the length of four cars.

Going bananas

Some tree frogs live in banana trees. When bananas are picked and shipped around the world, some tree frogs may go with them. Look out for them next time you buy a bunch of bananas!

▶ Trinidad leaf frogs are very small. They can travel around the world hidden between the leaves of plants.

---

parachute sheet of cloth shaped like an umbrella used to make a safe jump from an aircraft

Curious croaks

Each **species** of frog has a different sounding croak. Some frogs are named after the sort of croak they make. There are bullfrogs, sheep frogs, barking frogs, and even banjo frogs!

▶ This fringe-lipped bat has caught a frog and is eating it.

Sounds of danger

Croaking can sometimes be dangerous for frogs. It tells other animals where they are.

The fringe-lipped bat from South America eats frogs. It listens out for their croaking sounds. A pond full of croaking frogs soon falls silent when this bat appears. No frog moves or makes a sound until the bat has flown away again.

species type of living animal or plant

Siren sounds

Sirens are salamanders that live in water. When the water dries up they burrow into the mud. They wrap up in a coat of slime to stay wet. They live like this for many months until the rain returns. When it rains and the pond fills with water again, the sirens come back to life.

If a **predator** tries to catch them, sirens make a yelping sound. Some may even make a barking noise!

Toad calls

Natterjack toads live in Europe. They may be Europe's noisiest amphibian. The male's croak can be heard for several kilometres. We would have to shout very loud to be heard over the same distance!

◀ Natterjack toads make a loud croak. It sounds like this: *rrrRup, rrrRup*.

Amphibians in danger

A number of amphibians are now very rare. Some may soon disappear for ever.

Under threat

The corroboree frog is bright yellow and black. It lives only in the Snowy Mountains of Australia. In the last few years nearly three quarters of them have disappeared. No one knows why. Perhaps humans and their animals have damaged the land where they live.

Missing toad

The golden toad, shown above, has not been seen in Central America since 1989. At that time scientists thought only eleven toads were left. Very sadly, this toad is now probably **extinct**.

▶ Salamanders and newts are popular pets. But taking them from the wild is bad for them. Many are now in danger of dying out.

extinct died out, never to return

Disappearing salamanders

The golden alpine salamander is in serious danger of dying out. People have drained away the water where they live in Italy. Because of this the salamanders are losing their **habitat**. People have also taken these salamanders from the wild to keep as pets.

Some European newts are also rare now. The southern crested newt is probably disappearing the fastest of all. Humans are changing and destroying their river habitats. The newts are finding it hard to **survive** there anymore.

Whatever happened to...?
Scientists first discovered the gastric-brooding frog (below) in 1973. But less than ten years later it had disappeared from the wild. What made these frogs extinct? Poisoned water? Or did a disease kill them? No one knows for sure.

habitat natural home of an animal or plant

Poisoned water

The poisons we use to kill insects and other pests end up in our rivers. Frogs and toads take in water through their skin. If there are poisons in the water, they take in those too.

Danger zone

Scientists are worried. Amphibians are disappearing. Since the 1960s, the number of amphibians has been going down each year.

We take amphibians from the wild for pets. We take more water from rivers than we did before. We also put poisons in our rivers and streams. These, and other things we do, have a bad effect on the amphibians that live around us.

larva (more than one are called larvae) young form of an animal that is very different from the adult

▼ If we do not take care of our ponds and rivers, more and more amphibians will die.

Danger from fish

People put mosquito fish (shown below) in some lakes to eat mosquito **larvae**. But the fish also gobble up the larvae of amphibians. Where this happens, fewer frogs and salamanders **survive** to become adults.

Amphibians and us

Amphibians have always amazed us with their bright colours, their poisons, and their incredible change from egg to adult.

They have been on Earth for much longer than we have. Humans have a lot to do to make things better for amphibians again. We still have much to learn about these incredible animals.

---

survive stay alive despite danger and difficulties

Find out more

Websites

BBC Nature
The 'Wildfacts' website is packed with photos and information about all sorts of animals.
www.bbc.co.uk/nature/animals

Enchanted Learning
The 'Animal Printout' page has pictures, activities, and information on lots of different amphibians.
www.enchanted learning.com/color ing/amphibians

UK Safari
The 'Amphibians' page has information and photos of UK frogs, newts, and toads.
www.uksafari.com/amphibians.htm

Books

Amphibian (Eyewitness Guides), Barry Clarke (Dorling Kindersley, 1998)
Animal Kingdom: Amphibians, Sally Morgan (Raintree, 2004)
Keeping Unusual Pets: Salamanders, Peter Heathcote (Heinemann Library, 2004)

World wide web

To find out more about amphibians you can search the Internet. Use keywords like these:

• "Chinese giant salamander"
• poisonous +newt
• "horned frog"

You can find your own keywords by using words from this book. The search tips on page 53 will help you find useful websites.

Search tips

There are billions of pages on the Internet. It can be difficult to find exactly what you are looking for. These tips will help you find useful websites more quickly:

- Know what you want to find out about
- Use simple keywords
- Use two to six keywords in a search
- Only use names of people, places, or things
- Put double quote marks around words that go together, for example "cane toad"

Where to search

Search engine
A search engine looks through millions of website pages. It lists all the sites that match the words in the search box. You will find the best matches are at the top of the list, on the first page.

Search directory
A person instead of a computer has sorted a search directory. You can search by keyword or subject and browse through the different sites. It is like looking through books on a library shelf.

Numbers of incredible creatures

Creatures (y-axis): Amphibians, Mammals, Reptiles, Birds, Fish, Arachnids, Molluscs, Insects

Number of species (approximate) (x-axis): 0, 20,000, 40,000, 60,000, 80,000, 100,000, 120,000, 140,000, 160,000, 180,000, 1,000,000

Glossary

antidote medicine given to make a poison safe

anti-freeze liquid that does not freeze at temperatures below 0 °C (32 °F)

breed produce young

caecilian ("say see-silly-un") burrowing amphibian that has no limbs

camouflage colours and patterns that match the background

carnivore animal that eats meat

extinct died out, never to return

feeler little fleshy flap of skin used to smell, taste, or touch

frogspawn jelly-like mass of frogs' eggs

gills delicate, feathery structures that allow some animals to breathe under water

gland part of the body that produces chemicals such as poisons or digestive juices

glide float through the air

habitat natural home of an animal or plant

larva (**more than one are called larvae**) young form of an animal that is very different from the adult

mate when a male and female animal come together to produce young

metamorphosis change from being a larva to being an adult

midwife nurse who helps babies to be born

mimic (noun) one living thing that can copy another living thing

nutrient substance found in food that is needed by the body to grow strong and healthy

oxygen one of the gases in air and water that all living things need

parachute sheet of cloth shaped like an umbrella used to make a safe jump from an aircraft

predator animal that kills and eats other animals

prey animal that is killed and eaten by other animals

rainforest forest that grows in warm parts of the world where there is a lot of rainfall

shed get rid of, or lose

species type of living animal or plant

sugar cane grassy plant that sugar
  comes from
survive stay alive despite danger
  and difficulties
tadpole young stage, or larva, of
  a frog, toad, newt, or salamander
thaw when ice or snow melts
tropical area in the world lying
  close to the Equator where it
  is wet and very warm
virus very tiny creature that
  causes some diseases
waterproof does not let in water
whirlwind column of air whirling
  round and round very fast

Index

Titles in the *Freestyle Express*: *Incredible Creatures* series include:

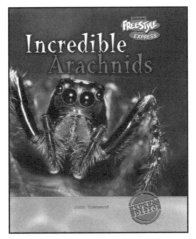

Hardback: 1844 434516

Hardback: 1844 434524

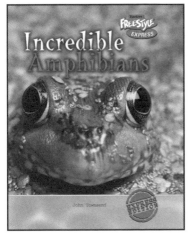

Hardback: 1844 434532

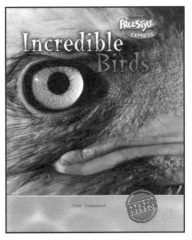

Hardback: 1844 434540

Hardback: 1844 434761

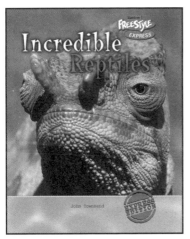

Hardback: 1844 43477X

Hardback: 1844 435172

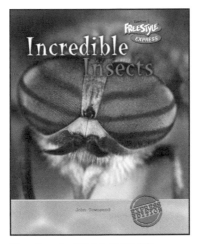

Hardback: 1844 435180

Find out about other Freestyle Express titles on our website www.raintreepublishers.co.uk